For Sophie and Georgia – may they grow to be strong women like their mother and grandmother.

The paintings in this book were inspired by the French and Australian impressionist painters Pierre-Auguste Renoir, Claude Monet, Fred McCubbin and Arthur Streeton. These artists were at their peak when our story was set in the late 1800s. They inspire me every day.

A Lothian Children's Book

Published in Australia and New Zealand in 2022
by Hachette Australia
Gadigal Country, Level 17, 207 Kent Street, Sydney NSW 2000
www.hachettechildrens.com.au

Hachette Australia acknowledges and pays our respects to the past,
present and future Traditional Owners and Custodians of Country
throughout Australia and recognises the continuation of cultural, spiritual
and educational practices of Aboriginal and Torres Strait Islander peoples.
Our head office is located on the lands of the Gadigal people
of the Eora Nation.

1 3 5 7 9 10 8 6 4 2

Text and illustrations copyright © Mark Wilson 2022

This book is copyright. Apart from any fair dealing for the purposes of private study, research,
criticism or review permitted under the *Copyright Act 1968*, no part may be stored or reproduced
by any process without prior written permission. Enquiries should be made to the publisher.

A catalogue record for this book is available from the National Library of Australia

ISBN 978 0 7344 2013 8 (hardback)

Designed by Christabella Designs
Colour reproduction by Splitting Image
Printed in China by Toppan Leefung Printing Limited

Her father eventually married again, and Nellie's stepmother, Rose, proved to be a strong-willed, determined woman. Nellie looked up to her. It wasn't easy taking over a household that included six children, but Rose just got on with the job.

Nellie loved the world she found herself in, sitting with her stepmother, as women gathered at their house and talked excitedly about women's rights and safety.

Her father eventually married again, and Nellie's stepmother, Rose, proved to be a strong-willed, determined woman. Nellie looked up to her. It wasn't easy taking over a household that included six children, but Rose just got on with the job.

Nellie loved the world she found herself in, sitting with her stepmother, as women gathered at their house and talked excitedly about women's rights and safety.

They wanted to help women experiencing poverty, domestic violence, and those who suffered terrible, cramped working conditions.

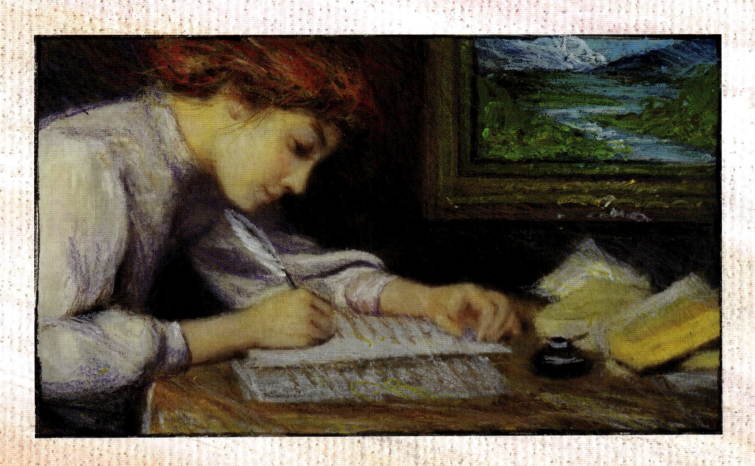

As Nellie took on more responsibilities in the household, she also became aware of the issues that women faced. She gladly went with Rose to meetings, and helped compose letters to the newspapers about these issues.

...and that for real reform to be achieved, women need to have the right to vote. Our voices need to be heard by those who make the laws.

One afternoon, as Nellie was writing a letter, she looked up to see a woman standing there. 'My dear girl, you have beautiful writing,' the woman said. 'My name is Mary Lee, and I would like you to write on a banner for me.'

Mary told Nellie the words to write on the banner and brought her a short length of silk to use. Then she smiled and said, 'One day, young lady, I promise you, we will stand together with this banner and cast our votes, with the rights that we are fighting for today.'

Nellie never forgot that promise. She didn't know it at the time, but history was being made. In 1888, the Women's Suffrage League was formed and it would be a huge force for change. Mary Lee was its Secretary, and Nellie's stepmother Rose became its hardworking Treasurer.

These were difficult times in the colony of South Australia. The collapse of the Commercial Bank and other businesses had led to widespread unemployment and many people were living in poverty.

Nellie, Rose and Mary helped where they could, while still working for women's rights.

Each day, Nellie was busier than ever – attending public meetings, writing letters and spreading the word with Rose and Mary about what they wanted to achieve: Votes for Women! Or in the words of the politicians and lawmakers, 'female suffrage'. The women had become suffragists!

Nellie sat in awe as Mary spoke eloquently about women's rights at social gatherings and public meetings. Mary even met with South Australian politicians!

Nellie felt so proud to be part of the Women's Suffrage League. They were not only lobbying for women to be allowed to vote, but also for children's rights. They began visiting factories where women worked in terrible conditions. They also organised food and clothing for the poor and destitute...

and, all the while, their campaign grew.

As Nellie sat discussing the campaign with Rose one bright autumn morning, Mary Lee arrived with some exciting news. The society had begun collecting signatures on a petition, and one day they would present it to parliament. They already had over a hundred signatures. The three friends set out to collect more signatures that afternoon...

and the petition grew, and grew, and grew!

More letters were written to newspapers and magazines. Trips around the colony were organised, meetings held and speeches made. Discussions were held with important political figures.

There was opposition to their cause and some meetings became rowdy. But the petition kept growing. It was now so big, it had to be rolled up carefully and tied with a ribbon to be carried from meeting to meeting.

One late winter afternoon, Nellie came home to find her stepmother waiting at the gate, looking very happy.

'Mary has some wonderful news!' Rose said excitedly. 'We now have thousands of signatures on the petition! Mary is going to hold a rally later this afternoon. We will try to get the total number of signatures to 10,000, or possibly more!'

Nellie and Rose went to the rally, and there was pandemonium.
They managed to get through the crowd to where Mary Lee stood.
When Mary started talking, many clapped and cheered...
But something wasn't right.

Not everyone was cheering, but there were always some people in
the crowd who were against women getting the right to vote.

This time, however, some of them were becoming angry.

Some people were shouting at Mary Lee. One man yelled, 'Go home where you belong!' Then another shouted, 'You women should be ashamed of yourselves!' There was pushing and shoving, then, without warning, a man fell against Rose.

It all happened in seconds. Nellie saw Rose fall and cry out.

Nellie and Mary went to help her up and guide her to a park bench not far away. 'Are you all right?' Nellie kept asking, until Rose replied softly, 'Please take me home.'

As the crowd broke up, the three women slowly made their way down Augusta Street towards home.

September 2, 1894.

Our huge petition, measuring 400 feet long, was presented to the South Australian House of Assembly on August 23, 1894. We had collected more than 11,600 signatures, a third of them from men. The petition was officially tabled on August 30. It called for equal rights for women, specifically ~~the right~~ to vote. This is a very ~~important~~ ~~moment~~ for us. We have put ~~our hearts into~~ ~~getting~~ this to ...

PETITION.

To the Honorable the Speaker and Members of the <u>House of Assembly</u> of South Australia, in Parliament assembled:

The petition undersigned <u>Adult Residents</u> in the province of South Australia, humbly sheweth:——

1. That your petitioners are convinced of the absolute justice of <u>giving Women the Franchise for both Houses of Parliament,</u> on the <u>same terms as</u> it is now, or hereafter be granted <u>to men.</u>

11. They therefore respectfully pray that the necessary Legislation may be passed by your Honorable <u>House with the least possible delay.</u>

And your Petitioners as in duty bound will ever pray, &e.

NAME.	ADDRESS.
J. S. Green.	Andamooka
H. E. Cummings	Andamooka
F. Thompson	Andamooka

The Constitution Amendment Act, giving South Australian women the right to vote, was finally passed on 18 December 1894. Over 200 women were present, clapping and cheering loudly.

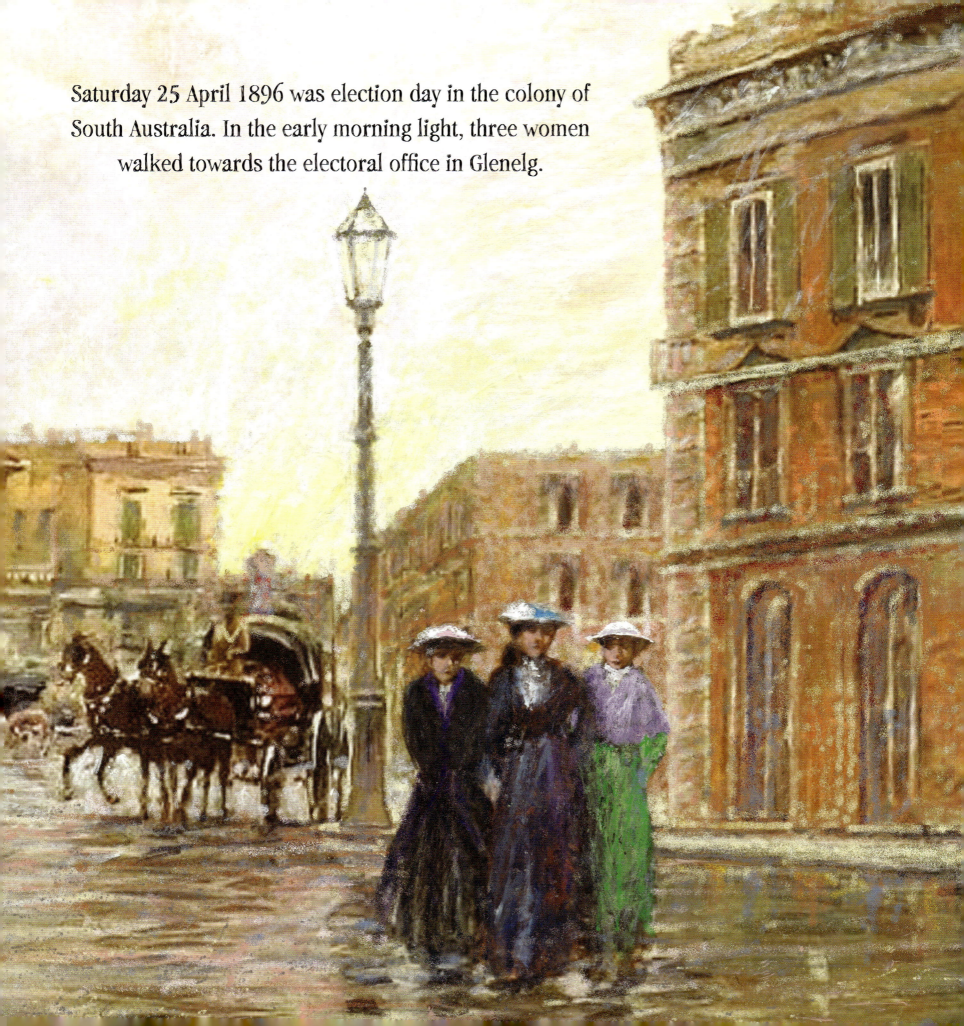
Saturday 25 April 1896 was election day in the colony of South Australia. In the early morning light, three women walked towards the electoral office in Glenelg.

At the top of the steps, Nellie, Rose and Mary hugged each other and entered the electoral office. Nellie then unfolded the silk banner, and Mary Lee helped her raise it up. The promise had been kept.

Rose smiled as she stepped forward and voted. Then, as she turned around, a tear came to her eye. The crowd that had gathered began to clap and cheer, including her stepdaughter Nellie, and her friend Mary Lee. Then, one by one, the women of South Australia stepped forward to lodge their first votes.

After three unsuccessful and frustrating attempts by women to gain equal voting rights, the South Australian Parliament finally passed the *Constitution Amendment (Adult Suffrage) Act* on 18 December 1894. South Australia was the first state in Australia to give women the right to vote, and the first in the whole world to give women the right to stand for election to parliament.

Rosetta 'Rose' Birks was the first woman to lodge her vote in Glenelg, South Australia on 25 April 1896. Nellie Fisher (nee Birks), who had spent her childhood and young adult life helping her stepmother and Mary Lee fight for women's rights, was the ninety-third person to sign the petition, and one of the first to vote.

Mary Lee was a tireless leader and the driving force behind the women's suffrage movement in South Australia, but she happily admitted, 'I could not have done it alone.'

'If I die before it is achieved ... "Women's enfranchisement" shall be found engraved upon my heart.' Mary Lee